Table of Contents

Introduction

Until the terrorist attacks of September 11, 2001, military officers were expected to focus on the pursuit and perfection of one common goal; the effective management of violence.[1] Requisite fundamental skills were honed in training throughout the cold war and applied in concert during the Vietnam and Gulf wars. While these two wars garnered polar results in terms of a tangible win or loss, the men who fought them shared the same heritage, national origin and culture. Of these two wars, Desert Storm emerged as a triumphant victory due in part to the applicable and rigorous training of military professionals prior to the initiation of hostilities.[2] From the end of Desert Storm through the beginning of Operation Iraqi Freedom, U.S. forces provided protection for the Kurdish population in Northern Iraq in the form of no fly zones that complemented an indirect approach to reconstruction of the region. The protection of Northern Iraqi Kurdistan led to an emergent *perception* of military intent by the people of Northern Iraq that evolved through future contact. The results in the second incursion into Iraq were vastly different. The initial invasion and toppling of the Iraqi regime by U.S. forces was reminiscent of their last meeting; however, the subsequent emergence of a counterinsurgency quickly overshadowed early success. In Northern Iraq, military leaders began to use money to shape and influence local initiatives to help quell the violence.[3] In Mosul, Iraq, the approximately 27,000 soldiers of the 101st Air Assault Division and their commander Major General Petraeus spent $57,668,710 on projects throughout the northern four provinces in the first nine months of 2003 in an effort to help shape the economic environment.[4] As the Army found itself in unfamiliar

---

[1] Samuel P. Huntington, *The Soldier and the State* (New York: Vintage Books, 1957), 11.
[2] Williamson Murray and Major General Robert H. Scales, *The Iraq War* (Cambridge: Belknap Press, 2003), 362-63.
[3] Colonel Michael Meese, "Economic Theory and the Need for Expeditionary Economics" (lecture, Fort Leavenworth, KS, April 12, 2010).
[4] Ibid.

territory, charged with the development of a failed economy, Colonel Michael Meese recalls the conflicted emergent requirements:

> When I was in Mosul in 2003, we implemented an extremely aggressive program of CERP (Commander's Emergency Response Program) spending—in fact pioneered many of the procedures. In total the U.S. forces employed 15,702 Iraqis who were entirely dependent on and thankful for the Coalition. When the Division of 20,000 soldiers commanded by a Major General was replaced by 6,000 soldiers in a Brigade Commanded by a Colonel and then 2,000 of those soldiers were deployed elsewhere, the continuity of support was lost and the loyalties of many in Mosul were up for grabs. Forces that were hostile to the coalition and the interim government took advantage of the situation and soon moved in and literally bought allegiances from many in the population. The Mayor of Mosul, who had been cooperating with Coalition Forces and had some influence, was assassinated and the city became a warzone. Certainly some other aspects of the counterinsurgency approach contributed to this situation, but the lack of sustainment of economic policies certainly did not help the situation.[5]

This is a clear example of the inherent risk associated with a professional military force shaping the economic environment while simultaneously saddled with the expectation to perform one of their core tasks, such as wide area security, throughout multiple regions.[6] While there are risks associated with any military operation, this study will explore the risks related to expeditionary economics and the viability of expeditionary economics as a military operation.

Expeditionary economics is an emerging economic field focused on rebuilding economies in post-conflict nations such as Iraq and Afghanistan. This concept has also been applied to the rebuilding of nations devastated by natural disasters; however, the focus of this study will search the realm of conflict where prolonged military presence is required or expected and where the local environment is in desperate need of stabilization and economic development. Initially, this concept was theorized by Dr. Schramm in an essay in the May/June 2010 issue of *Foreign Affairs*.[7] His thesis states that expeditionary economics is the most effective way to quickly establish positive economic growth in areas of conflict by mobilizing capitalistic

---

[5] Colonel Michael Meese, "Economic Theory and the Need for Expeditionary Economics" (lecture, Fort Leavenworth, KS, October 1, 2011).

[6] U.S. Army, *Army Doctrinal Publication 3-0, Unified Land Operations* (Washington DC: Headquarters, Department of the Army, 2011), 2.

[7] C. J. Schramm, "Expeditionary Economics," *Foreign Affairs* (May/June 2010): 89-99.

initiatives. These initiatives potentially gain a foothold in an identified market segment through the presence and stability efforts of U.S. forces. The premise of this discipline places considerable weight on a military response, but does not appear to be developed in terms of understanding the potential risks that emerge by utilizing the military at the forefront of primary economic development efforts. The current expeditionary economics theory particularly fails to address the complexities of unviable war- torn economies. It further lacks the emphasis on the importance of *understanding the local environment* and how local *perception* of any U.S. military action is deeply rooted in historical interaction both direct and indirect.

This monograph is organized into five sections. Section one provides an introduction and comprehensive literature review of pertinent works on expeditionary economics as well as a list of definitions. Section two then examines two specific case studies that will be evaluated with a common framework from the Alexander George case study methodology.[8] The theory building research objective chosen for this study is the building block technique which studies common patterns in heuristic studies.[9] It will aim to identify patterns and fill gaps in understanding the risk of employing expeditionary economics with military forces in two unrelated examples. Required military tasks within Stability Operations will provide a foundation of tasks that military units are prepared for in training, mitigating some of the risk. This broad-spanning study will provide a coherent and systematic comparison utilizing a three-step approach for each case study.[10] First, each crisis is described in detail and given a historical context. Second, critical interests are identified as they relate to U.S. national interests which may or may not warrant the involvement of U.S. military forces. Third, analysis of each crisis addresses several specific questions: Who leads or influences economic change in the conflict, and are those efforts aligned with U.S.

---

[8] Alexander L. George, Andrew Bennett, *Case Studies and Theory Development in the Social Sciences* (Cambridge: MIT Press, 2005), 65.
[9] Ibid., 76.
[10] Ibid., 301.

national interest, how are economic advisors integrated into stability operations and what is their degree of influence, and were there unintended consequences (second and third order effects) of military led economic development? The case studies used to support this monograph were selected based upon their fragile political status and the protracted involvement of U.S. military action.

Methodology

The objective of this monograph is to examine the use of U. S. military forces serving a lead role in the employment of expeditionary economics through a case study analysis, focusing on the operational risk involved as a result of military-led economic intervention. These risks potentially pose a direct threat to the achievement of national strategic objectives due to an increased role in economic development by military forces ill-suited to the task. This monograph will focus on contemporary case studies that are significant and similar in that they both are examples of fragile states which experienced U.S. military intervention. These types of environments where stability operations are employed in the midst of continuous conflict appear to be the norm for the intervention of U. S. military forces over the past two decades. These complex environments pose new challenges and necessitate the creative employment of military force in nontraditional roles, which leads to emergent risks.

There are at least three risks associated with placing a heavy burden of economic development squarely on the shoulders of a professional military force. The first is the inability to maintain contact and influence within the area of concern due to competing wide area security requirements as earlier portrayed by the experience of Colonel Meese in Iraq. Providing security constitutes one of the primary U.S. military missions according to current doctrine, and is a task that falls within their professional identity. There is perhaps a fine line between economy of force and an ineffectual effort to achieve a clear strategic goal or objective. While comparing the skills of military officers versus other professions, Samuel P. Huntington differentiates the function of a military force as one that is successful in armed combat.[11]   He describes the skill of a military officer as "an extraordinarily complex intellectual skill requiring comprehensive study and

---

[11] Huntington, *The Soldier and the State*, 26.

5

training."[12] He further emphasizes those variations in levels of responsibility noting that a leader of a platoon does not possess or require the requisite skills of a division commander in charge of thousands.[13]

The second risk is the threat that tasking military units to conduct economic interventions may threaten the delicate balance of political and military subordination that is required to ensure economic efforts are in line with national policy. This study is not conducted from a position that advocates a stove pipe approach to policy application; however, blending the elements of diplomatic, information, military, and economic powers into a single expeditionary organization inherently appears risky as it moves tasks normally for the Department of State and USAID to the Department of Defense. This is the potential concern associated with utilizing uniformed military forces in a broader role that includes economic development without substantial cooperation of interagency professionals and experts. It is appropriate to highlight and to be mindful of the United States traditions of proper subordination of military effort to political will and to expose the potential risks associated with unilateral military execution of what are historically clear governmental responsibilities. The classical theorist Carl von Clausewitz, reminds us of this delicate relationship in his writings. "War is only a branch of political activity that … is in no sense autonomous … The only source of war is politics – the intercourse of governments and peoples… War cannot be divorced from political life; and whenever this occurs in our thinking about war, the many links that connect the two elements are destroyed and we are left with something pointless and devoid of sense."[14] As this relates to the forces that execute war, it may be equivalently risky for a military force to embark on expeditionary economic efforts without significant political directive coupled with comprehensive means and adequate military

---

[12] Huntington, *The Soldier and the State*, 11-13.
[13] Ibid, 12.
[14] Michael Howard, Peter Paret. *Carl Von Clausewitz: On War* (New Jersey: Princeton University Press, 1976), 605.

representation that is capable of influencing change.[15] Understanding the language of risk and how it is measured by a professional military is important to assessing the challenges of employing expeditionary economics.

The third risk is one of *perception*. Contemporary historical examples from Vietnam to Operation Iraqi Freedom illustrate the U.S. military's expertise in the massive use of force to achieve military objectives. The military efforts in these two examples varied from counterinsurgency to search and destroy missions to major combat operations which created an initial impression upon the local population and the world as to the role of uniformed soldiers.[16] This perception manifested itself into a positive or negative impression of military forces which set the stage for future expectations of their assumed role by the populations it interfaced within both cases. It may be problematic for an armed and uniformed military force to effectively shift roles into an economic building capacity and create a new narrative as to their current intentions and their future ambitions. Even if the military can complete this transition, the willingness of the local population to accept them in this new role may be limited, affecting mission effectiveness.

The case studies are presented in order of increasing military involvement in Stability Operations and involvement in tasks that align with expeditionary economic ideas and concepts. The first case study will focus on and evaluate a limited military response directly after the second civil war in Liberia from 2002 to 2004. This case study is exceptionally unique because it involved a local regional initiative that was responsible for economic development known as the Economic Community of West African States (ECOWAS). The ECOWAS also employed a distinct military element to help achieve regional objectives. The second case study will evaluate risks in a limited military intervention environment and focus on the conduct of stability

---

[15] John P. Kotter, *Power and Influence* (New York: Free Press, 1985), 12.
[16] Lewis Sorley. *A Better War: The Unexamined Victories and Final Tragedy of America's Last Years in Vietnam* (Orlando: Harvest Book Hartcourt, Inc., 2008), 21.

operations in Somalia from 1992 to 1994. This case will provide a historical example of traditional stability roles while evaluating the execution of expeditionary economic initiatives.

Section five will provide a conclusion that identifies the clear operational risks that emerge from the research and deliver a feasible recommendation for military force involvement in expeditionary economics. Recommendations will suggest that the Army incorporate concepts of economic awareness and the impact of economic operations on the environment into the Army's Composite Risk Management Field Manual. Recommendations will address operational risk mitigation as it relates to the employment of economic development in stability operations.

Literature Review

Risk Defined

The U.S. Army identifies risk as a composite hazard that has the potential to injure or kill personnel, damage or destroy equipment, or otherwise impact mission effectiveness.[17] Through a focused effort, the Army has attempted to significantly reduce risk through the use of composite risk management employed through deliberate planning. The Composite Risk Field Manual (FM 5-19) gives specific examples of simple tactical risk mitigation for concerns such as basic vehicular ground guiding; however, there is little reference to much more complex operational risks that emerge as a result of attempting to solve ill-structured problems such as stability and economic development. The development of economies certainly falls within the realm of an ill-structured problem. The problem is as diverse and complex as understanding differences in individual and blended cultures; it necessitates a comprehensive understanding of the written and unwritten rules of the environment upon which the application is desired.[18] Current doctrine does not address the physical comprehensive requirements in terms of equipment, manning, and training that would be required to accomplish an expeditionary economic role. Without this framework, it is difficult to assess and control the emergent risk of such an important mission. One of the emergent requirements of expeditionary economics as an independent discipline is the identification of a requisite organizational structure and training requirement.[19]

---

[17] U.S. Army, *Field Manual (FM) 5-19, Composite Risk Management* (Washington DC: Headquarters, Department of the Army, 2006), 6.

[18] Everett C. Dolman, *Pure Strategy: Power and Principle in the Space and Information Age* (New York: Frank Cass, 2005), 90. According to Dolman, "True strategic power is the capacity to manipulate shared understanding of rules, norms and other boundaries that set parameters in action."

[19] C.J. Schramm, "Expeditionary Economics," *Foreign Affairs* (May/June 2010): 89-99.

Economic Theory

In order to understand the vast complexities of the term economics, it is important to provide a foundational understanding of the history, terminology, and the ambitions of expeditionary economics. The term economics in its most basic form is "the study of the behavior of human beings in producing, distributing, and consuming material goods and services in a world of scarce resources."[20] This contemporary definition is the result of historical evolution based on state policies guided in part by accredited pioneers of the discipline. There are numerous theorists and governmental techniques throughout history that are instructive regarding the application of policies today.

Early theoretical economic writings from the sixteenth and seventeenth centuries discuss a government-centric style of policies known as Mercantilism. This term was first coined by the Count de Mirabeau in 1763 and addressed the governmental control of trade in order to secure state interests.[21] Mercantilism encouraged importation of cheap raw materials to be used in manufacturing goods, which could be exported, and, for state regulation, to impose protective tariffs on foreign manufactured goods and prohibit manufacturing in the colonies. This control was later criticized by Adam Smith who denounced policies that encouraged monopolies over trade with colonial interests which in turn led to an increased cost militarily to secure those interests.[22]

The subsequent critiques by Adam Smith formed a historical transition in economic thought through his writings in *The Wealth of Nations* published in 1776. This evolutionary publication led to the independent standing of economics as a separate discipline within the social

---

[20] Campbell R. McConnell and Stanley L. Brue, *Economics: Principles, Problems, and Policies*, (New York: McGraw-Hill, 2004), 1.
[21] Henry William Spiegel, *The Growth of Economic Thought* (Washington DC: Library of Congress, 1991), 93.
[22] Jerry Z. Muller, *Adam Smith in his Time and Ours* (New York: Free Press, 1993), 84.

sciences.[23] The book identified land, labor, and capital as the three factors of production and the major contributors to a nation's wealth. In Smith's view, the ideal economy is a self-regulating market system that automatically satisfies the economic needs of the populace. He described the self-regulatory market mechanism as an "invisible hand" that leads all individuals, in pursuit of their own self-interests, to produce the greatest benefit for society as a whole.[24] His foundational views of economic principles hold contemporary relevance to economists much like the foundational theoretical views of Clausewitz's *On War* are applicable to military planners today.

John Maynard Keynes is a name that most would recognize and attribute to economic theory. His work throughout the twentieth century is relied upon today and was particularly influential during the Great Depression and World War II.[25] Keynes attempted to explain economic problems with the use of a model that states that output in the economy will be determined by consumption, investment, and government demand for goods and services.[26] Similar to Mercantilism, Keynes supported government intervention in the economy as necessary to ensure the overall health of the economy. However, he diverges from mercantilism when he argues that encouraging production was just as important as consumption. His theories and personal guidance assisted policymakers in their navigating the treacherous economic waters of the first half of the twentieth century. Since his death in 1946, many U.S. policymakers have been influenced by Keynesian principles to include the Obama administration whose 2008 stimulus package mirrored his framework.

Keynesian economics has six basic tenants according to Alan Butler, a professor of economics at Princeton University:

------

[23] Muller, *Adam Smith in his Time and Ours*, 3-7.
[24] Ibid., 86.
[25] David McCord Wright, *The Keynesian System* (New York: Fordham University Press, 1961), 1.
[26] Ibid., 4.

1. A Keynesian believes that aggregate demand is influenced by a host of economic decisions—both public and private—and sometimes behaves erratically.

2. According to Keynesian theory, changes in aggregate demand, whether anticipated or unanticipated, have their greatest short-run effect on real output and employment, not on prices.

3. Keynesians believe that prices, and especially wages, respond slowly to changes in supply and demand, resulting in periodic shortages and surpluses, especially of labor.

4. Keynesians do not think that the typical level of unemployment is ideal—partly because unemployment is subject to the caprice of aggregate demand, and partly because they believe that prices adjust only gradually.

5. Many, but not all, Keynesians advocate activist stabilization policy to reduce the amplitude of the business cycle, which they rank among the most important of all economic problems.

6. Finally, and even less unanimously, some Keynesians are more concerned about combating unemployment than about conquering inflation. [27]

As Keynesian economics theory grew and became more widely accepted, another economic theory known as the Chicago School of economics emerged to counter its principles. This effort was pioneered by a professor named Milton Friedman who advocated for free markets and rejected the use of fiscal policy as a healthy government action. He blamed the Keynesian model for the severity of the Great Depression noting that the government's hand in the contraction of the monetary supply has only worsened the crisis.[28] Another opponent to the Keynesian model was Friedrich von Hayek who drew attention to the lack of information necessary to positively affect economies through central control. He authored *The Road to*

---

[27] Alan S. Blinder, "Keynsian Economics: The Concise Encyclopedia of Economics," *The Library of Economics and Liberty*, http://www.econlib.org/library/Enc/KeynesianEconomics.html (accessed November 16, 2011).
[28] Daniel Yergin and Joseph Stanislaw, *The Commanding Heights* (New York City, Free Press, 1998), 127-128.

Serfdom and argued that the price system was a means of communicating information about the markets.[29] While Hayek was not a member of the Chicago school of economics, he purportedly greatly influenced the thought and development of Friedman.[30]

These are the principle theorists whose economic models influence our currently fiscal policies in both domestic and international efforts. Recent efforts by the United States in Afghanistan to engage in nation-building have led to ongoing debate as to which models should be effectively employed. One of the inherent risks in disjointed efforts to promote economic stability or growth is the threat of inadvertently supporting terrorist activity.

> Terrorist finance generally involves relatively small and irregular transactions of funds often derived from legitimate activities but put to severely destructive ends. Al Qaeda, for example, has used a variety of channels to transfer funds for its operations, including smuggling cash, gold, and diamonds; hawala, a traditional money transfer system; the inadequately regulated Islamic financial system; and wire transfers and other instruments used by modern Western financial systems."[31]

This illustrates the looming risk of forfeiting well intentioned economic initiatives to the hands of enemy forces. While U.S. military forces are well prepared to conduct doctrinal tasks such as wide area security and combined arms maneuver, they are not commonly prepared to apply complex economic theories to war torn environments. Well intentioned attempts to provide stability through economics by an untrained entity, may lead to disastrous second and third order effects. The journey to provide stability to a region must be planned carefully and consider local *perceptions* of foreign intent and intervention. It must also apply the correct theories with the proper economic tools after a comprehensive *understanding of the environment* is obtained.

---

[29] Daniel Yergin and Joseph Stanislaw, *The Commanding Heights* (New York City, Free Press, 1998), 125.
[30] Milton & Rose Friedman, *Two Lucky People: Memoirs* (Chicago: Chicago Press, 1998), 333.
[31] Marcus Noland and Howard Pack, *The Arab Economies in a Changing World* (Washington: Peter G. Peterson Institute for International Economics, 2007), 118.

13

Expeditionary Economics

The U.S. Army's *Field Manual 3-07, Stability Operations* outlines the importance of collaborative efforts to stabilize local economies in the aftermath of war or natural disaster. The current role for military forces within decisive action is twofold. The first effort is the infrastructure assessment as associated with the restoration of essential services and the second is infrastructure survey which supports economic and infrastructure development.[32] The military role is classically designed around the capability to provide firsthand reports and information through reconnaissance. This is currently only intended to rapidly improve essential services in order to reduce tensions and create interim stability.

Focused economic initiative requirements may create a significant pressure on military forces as they attempt to coordinate and balance simultaneous efforts along Political, Military, Economic, Social, Infrastructure, Information, Physical Environment, and Time (PMESII-PT) operational variables. Pressures form to ensure that economic initiatives as identified and introduced to the area of operations are valid and focused on the long-term development of the community. Additionally, there is pressure to ensure that initiatives do not morph into or support illicit trade and production activities for products such as opium in Afghanistan or weapons smuggling in Iraq. Most substantially, there is pressure to provide additional security forces for the protection and development of projects from their initiation through their sustainment of operations. This also requires the aforementioned requisite leadership level to maintain long-term responsibility and continuity to the local or regional effort assigned. While it is critical that a strategy is developed for achieving post-conflict growth and stability, independent operational risks emerge along numerous variables as a result of economic initiatives employed by warfighters whose primary professional competencies lie in the realm of warfighting.

---

[32] U.S. Army, *Field Manual (FM) 3-07, Stability Operations* (Washington DC: Headquarters, Department of the Army, 2009), 2-12.

U.S. Army Stability Operations Doctrine (FM 3-07) provides definitions and unifying concepts that potentially enable expeditionary economics through the use of either the whole of government approach or what is alternatively termed a comprehensive approach.[33] Both of these approaches recognize the importance of Department of Defense integration while neither explicitly recommends unilateral effort from any one organization. The primary focus for the military component is described and practiced today in stability operations. Lines of effort for stability operations are clearly defined in doctrine and in fact include economic stabilization; however, what is not clear is the specific role U.S. military forces should play in the economic rebuilding process. It is important to remember that every conflict is unique as is the role military forces are required to play in those conflicts. Clarity must be sought in this matter, especially in the midst of increased action in areas of responsibility that includes one or more fragile states where the *environment is misunderstood* and local *perceptions* of military actions are weary.

---

[33] U.S. Army, *Field Manual (FM) 3-07, Stability Operations* (Washington DC: Headquarters, Department of the Army, 2009), 2-12.

Liberia

"Causation is a vexed issue in West African wars. Some observers label the fighting as unfathomable chaos, and others regard it as a natural response to economics and other factors. Many people throw up their hands, acknowledging that it is perhaps impossible to explain why matters took place the way they did."[34]

History

Liberia which literally means land of the free was founded in 1820 by freed African-American slaves from the United States. A small group of immigrants established a settlement in the area now known as Monrovia which was named after U.S. President James Monroe.[35] Early appropriations from Congress topped one hundred thousand dollars in 1819 for the establishment of Liberia by the American Colonization Society which in today's dollars equates to an over two billion dollar investment.[36] It is already easy to see the lineage of importance and influence upon which the United States places its interests in that region. The United States officially recognized Liberia in 1862 and its Americo-Liberian leadership. It later shared a strategic relationship with Liberia during the Cold War.[37] The area of primary interests for this study focuses on two areas. The first is the decade that leads up to the first civil war which is portrayed as significantly important to the strategic and economic interests of the United States. Secondly, is the first period of civil conflict and its emergence from that conflict through the aid of the Economic Community of West African States (ECOWAS).

---

[34]The Economist, "War and Peace in Monrovia," The Economist Library, http://www.economist.com/blogs/prospero/2012/02/war-and-peace-monrovia?fsrc=gn_ep (accessed November 16, 2011).

[35] U.S. Department of State, "Background Note: Liberia," Bureau of African Affairs, http://www.state.gov/r/pa/ei/bgn/6618.htm (accessed November 16, 2011).

[36] According to the U.S. Department of State, "Liberia by the American Colonization Society led by prominent Americans such as Francis Scott Key, George Washington's nephew Bushrod, Henry Clay, Daniel Webster, and Presidents Monroe (for whom Liberian settlers named the capital, Monrovia), Adams, and Jackson." U.S. Department of State, "Background Note: Liberia," Bureau of African Affairs, http://www.state.gov/r/pa/ei/bgn/6618.htm (accessed November 16, 2011).

[37] Ibid.

Conditions for the first civil war were set in the unstable decade of 1980. A rebel army emerged as the National Patriotic Front of Liberia (NPFL), led by the standing president Samuel Kanyon Doe's former procurement chief Charles Taylor. Five years after fleeing Liberia, on December 24, 1989 Taylor and the NPFL invaded Liberia from Cote d'Ivoire.[38] Taylor and his rebels rapidly gained the support of many Liberians who were exhausted by the brutality of the nine year presidency of Doe.[39] From that point and up until 1996, one of Africa's bloodiest civil wars ensued, claiming the lives of more than 200,000 Liberians and displacing a million others into refugee camps in neighboring countries.[40] ECOWAS intervened with the help of its military arm, the economic community monitoring group (ECOMOG), in 1990 and succeeded in preventing Charles Taylor from capturing Monrovia. To further complicate the unstable environment, a former member of Taylor's NPFL, Prince Johnson, formed a break-away faction known as the Independent National Patriotic Front of Liberia (INPFL).[41] Johnson's forces captured and killed Doe on September 9, 1990. Taking refuge in Sierra Leone and other neighboring countries, former Armed Forces of Liberia (AFL) soldiers founded the new insurgent United Liberation Movement of Liberia for Democracy (ULIMO), fighting back Taylor's NPFL.[42]

Economically, Liberia was always known for its iron-mining, and rubber plantations. The political upheavals that began in the 1980s coupled with a 14-year civil war (1989-2003) destroyed Liberia's economy and casused a steep decline in living standards. The Liberian economy relied heavily on the mining of iron ore and on the export of natural rubber prior to the

---

[38] Mark Huband, *The Liberian Civil War* (London: Frank Cass Publishers, 1998), xvi.
[39] Ibid.
[40] U.S. Department of State, "Background Note: Liberia," Bureau of African Affairs, http://www.state.gov/r/pa/ei/bgn/6618.htm (accessed November 16, 2011).
[41] Ibid.
[42] Ibid.

civil war.[43] Liberia was a major exporter of iron ore on the world market and in the 1970s and 1980s, iron mining accounted for more than half of Liberia's export earnings.[44] Following the coup d'état by Doe in 1980, the country's economic growth rate slowed because of a decline in the demand for iron ore on the world market and political upheavals in Liberia. Due to the unprecedented violence during the 1989-2003 civil war, most major businesses were destroyed or heavily damaged, and most foreign investors and businesses left the country.[45] A widely circulated article published in 1994 by Robert D. Kaplan in the *Atlantic Monthly*, describes his view of the desperate and seemingly hopeless environment present in the African region. He states that Liberia is "the symbol of worldwide demographic, environmental, and societal stress, in which criminal anarchy emerges as the real 'strategic' danger."[46] In the midst of this disparate societal environment, iron ore production stopped completely, and the United Nations banned timber and diamond exports from Liberia. As a result of political and economic instability, the county of Liberia was in desperate need for stabilization and reform.

Stabilization, aid and reform eventually came in the form of assistance from ECOWAS. In 1975, ECOWAS was formed with the objective of bringing economic and political unity to West Africa. Liberia was one of the fifteen founding members of ECOWAS.[47] The purpose of ECOWAS, as the African leaders envisioned it, was to foster the development of an economic union in the sub-region to "raise the living standards of its peoples, and to maintain and enhance

---

[43] U.S. Department of State, "Background Note: Liberia," Bureau of African Affairs, http://www.state.gov/r/pa/ei/bgn/6618.htm (accessed November 16, 2011).

[44] Elwood D. Dunn and Svend E. Holsoe, *Historical Dictionary of Liberia* (London: The Scarecrow Press, 1985), 92.

[45] U.S. Department of State, "Background Note: Liberia," Bureau of African Affairs, http://www.state.gov/r/pa/ei/bgn/6618.htm (accessed November 16, 2011).

[46] Robert D. Kaplan, "The Coming Anarchy," *The Atlantic Monthly* (February 1994): 44.

[47] "On May 28, 1975, heads of state and government of fifteen West African countries--Benin, Burkina Faso, Côte d'Ivoire, the Gambia, Ghana, Guinea, Guinea-Bissau, Liberia, Mali, Mauritania, Niger, Nigeria, Senegal, Sierra Leone, and Togo--convened in Lagos to sign the treaty establishing the Economic Community of West African States (ECOWAS)." *Economic Community of West African States Revised Treaty, 24 July 1993*, http://www.worldtradelaw.net/fta/agreements/ ecowasfta.pdf (accessed November 16,2011) 1.

economic stability, foster relations among Member States and contribute to the progress and

development of the African Continent."[48] ECOWAS called for cooperation in culture, commerce,

industry, transportation, scientific and technical research and training, medicine, public health and

nutrition.[49] One of its overarching goals was to bring together the economies of smaller regional

nations in an effort to compete globally and beyond the ability of any individual nation.[50] Other

goals contained under ECOWAS charter included the harmonization of national polices,

increased integration, common environmental protection policies, the creation of joint enterprises,

the formation of a common market, adoption of uniform trade policies, and the standardization of

legal practices. ECOWAS' primary stated mission remains to "promote co-operation and

integration in order to create an economic and monetary union for encouraging economic growth

and development in West Africa." Since its inception, the group has taken proactive roles by

working towards elimination of custom duties, establishing a common external tariff and creating

a uniform monetary unit.[51] These efforts are not only in the interests of the individual nations,

but also of the region. This is the reason ECOWAS has maintained a deliberate role in stability of

war torn internal regions such as Liberia.

Critical Interest Related to U.S. National Interests

In the 1980s, the United States and the members of the European Economic Community

(ESS–also known as the Common Market) were the principal customers for Liberia's exports

---

[48] Heads of State and Government of the Member States of the Economic Community of West African States (ECOWAS), "ECOWAS Treaty," http://www.worldtradelaw.net/fta/agreements/ecowasfta.pdf (accessed November 16,2011) 3.1.

[49] Elwood D. Dunn and Svend E. Holsoe, *Historical Dictionary of Liberia* (London: The Scarecrow Press, 1985), 64.

[50]PBS, "Liberia's Uneasy Peace," Economic Community of West African States, http://www.pbs.org/newshour/bb/africa/liberia/ecowas-background.html (accessed Novsmber 16, 2011).

[51] Heads of State and Government of the Member States of the Economic Community of West African States (ECOWAS) "ECOWAS Treaty," http://www.worldtradelaw.net/fta/agreements/ecowasfta.pdf , (accessed November 16,2011) 3.1.

with the United States'' share alone over twenty percent in 1981.[52] The primary goods involved in exports were shipments of iron ore and rubber by American and German controlled subsidiary companies in Liberia.[53] Iron ore quickly overcame the primary export of rubber and totaled more than sixty percent of the total exports in 1981.[54] At that time, the United States happened to garner the largest share of the Liberian iron ore market at fifty percent.[55] The United States and the partner EEC companies also contributed to the greater amount of Liberia's imports. In 1981 the United States private investment in Liberia was half a billion dollars, the third largest in African at the time. Large companies such as Firestone, Uniroyal, and Bethlehem Steel shared the majority of the interest. Loans and grants from the U.S. Agency for International Development (USAID) flooded the country and increased tenfold from 1980 to 1981.

Historically, additional U.S. interests in Liberia are broad in scope and tied not only to the development and sustainment of West African Nations, but to global interests as well. Regional interests during the period in question include Liberia serving as a base station for the Voice of America that served as a transmitter that broadcasts to all of Africa, the Middle East, and parts of Southwest Asia. Diplomatic interest in the form of hardware and capacity included the Telecommunications Relay Station which transmitted diplomatic traffic between Washington and more than forty embassies on the continent of Africa.[56] Liberia also served as a major maritime and air control interest included the OMEGA navigational station which served as part of a network of eight world-wide stations that enabled ships and aircraft to continuously calculate

---

[52] Harold D. Nelson. Liberia: *A Country Study* (Washington, DC: Foreign Area Studies The American University, 1984), 192.

[53] Ibid.

[54] Elwood D. Dunn and Svend E. Holsoe, *Historical Dictionary of Liberia* (London: The Scarecrow Press, 1985), 92.

[55] Ibid., 92.

[56] Ibid., 181.

their positions.[57] This is analogous to the importance of Global Positioning Systems today and their dependent satellite constellation's critical role in all forms of navigation that is vitally tied to the engine of international trade and commerce. At the time, Liberia served as the principle stopping point in all of Africa for Pan American Airways.[58] Pan Am was the principle and largest international air carrier in the United States from 1927 until its collapse on December 4, 1991.[59] These interests were supported and bolstered by the U.S. Military efforts as well.

The U.S. Military Mission (USMM) to Liberia existed at varying degrees and capacity since 1951.[60] Its primary role was the development of Liberia's defense capacity and effectiveness. It assisted in the development of planning, construction, training, maintenance, acquisition of equipment as well as civic action programs.[61] These efforts were derivatives of a broader U.S. effort to introduce programs such as the Military Aid Program (MAP), the Grant Aid Training and Foreign Military Sales, and the MAP Aid Equipment.[62] These initiatives certainly influenced the landscape of Liberia while potentially enabling the AFL to address national challenges prior to the civil war.

Economic Inquiries

The first question is "Who leads or influences economic change in the conflict, and are those efforts aligned with U.S. national interest?" The primary leader of economic change throughout the tumultuous era of civil war conflict in Liberia appears to be the ECOWAS organization. What makes this organization more effective for an unstable nation such as Liberia

---

[57] Elwood D. Dunn and Svend E. Holsoe, *Historical Dictionary of Liberia* (London: The Scarecrow Press, 1985), 92.
[58] Ibid.
[59] George E. Burns, "The Jet Age Arrives," Pan American Historical Foundation, http://runway.cloudaccess.net/stories/70-the-jet-age-arrives.html (accessed November 6, 2011)
[60] Elwood D. Dunn and Svend E. Holsoe, *Historical Dictionary of Liberia* (London: The Scarecrow Press, 1985), 181.
[61] Ibid.
[62] Ibid.

was the military arm of the organization known as ECOMOG. The clear distinction between ECOMOG intervention as a tool to enforce regional stability through the unified mandates of ECOWAS and a western power attempting to enforce a seemingly foreign policy with military boots on the ground was in the local perception. While the United States has long maintained economic interest in the region since the establishment of Liberia as an independent nation, it has done so primarily through the creditable regional organizations while bolstering its legitimacy and potential for success through the numerous military and government aid programs as discussed earlier.

The second question is "How are economic advisors integrated into stability operations and what is their degree of influence?" Advisors to Liberia came not only in the form of USAID specialists, but also regional ECOWAS partners who were concerned with maintaining their own interests. One of these influential neighbors was the country of Nigeria. It was clear that it wanted to portray itself as a regional leader and would extend its will through the use of troops under the unified ECOMOG charter. Nigeria felt threatened by the derogatory reports emanating from Liberia and echoing around the world.[63] It did not want to be associated with the growing worldwide prejudice against Liberia and risk the potential for mutual association in culture and policy. This would clearly hinder their ability to benefit economically from the growing surge of globalization.

The final question explored in this case study is "What were the unintended consequences (second and third order effects) of military led economic development?" Separatists involved in the coup d'état to overthrow the government arguably benefited from military training and equipment funded and sponsored by the United States. Regional ECOWAS partners have always maintained a more localized interest in preserving regional stability and thus

---

[63] Mark Huband, *The Liberian Civil War* (London: Frank Cass Publishers, 1998), 183.

reaped both the benefits of external aid while suffering the unintended consequences of indirect support to civil war belligerents. Historically, this interest was especially important to the local nation of Nigeria which did not want the negative image of Liberia to envelope its own identity.

ECOWAS provided training to help Liberia build capacity to defend itself and quell internal conflicts. This was achieved through their military arm, ECOMOG, which was well supported by the United States in terms of funding, equipment, and training. This training and resourcing that was exercised through the employment of contracts and capital opportunities provided to global businesses, potentially resulted in unintended consequences. The civil wars that wreaked havoc on the countryside for over a decade were initiated by individuals and ideas. The collective groups that they formed benefited from the military equipment sales and the training that was provided from external business opportunists. Images of young boys brandishing U.S. made M-16 assault rifles are not hard to find in literature that defines the violence of Liberia's civil war.

While the consequences of military employment of economic opportunities through equipping and training unintentionally supported internal uprisings, the true consequences lie in the macroeconomic impact of an unstable Liberia. Instability and internal strife gave way to an increase in production costs to commodities such as iron ore and rubber which previously served as the engine of economic activity in the country. The United Nation's enduring commitment to improve the overall conditions is described in one of their reports after the war: "The effects of economic mismanagement, corrupt government, administrative abuse and infrastructure collapse were compounded by the socio-economic and humanitarian impact of sanctions. The importance of this undertaking is hard to overestimate since any progress towards greater stability and

23

security depends on how quickly basic services are restored and the economic engine restarted."[64]

Those that argue the utility of expeditionary economics in a role that could bolster the country's ability to return to a stable and viable economy may be overcome with current insecurity conditions first. Additional risk associated with increased U.S. military involvement includes the potential to increase instability. This could occur due to a competing perception by competing factious organizations that U.S. military efforts are supporting one side or the other.

---

[64] United Nations Mission in Liberia, "Liberia: Development Challenges to Agenda as the Nation Recovers from Years of Civil Strife," United Nations, http://www.un.org/events/tenstories/06/story.asp?storyID=2100 (accessed November 16, 2011).

Somalia

My enthusiasm for the project (Aid and relief in Somalia) derived from my idealistic notion that economics was the best way to alleviate poverty. However, I learned fast in Somalia that insecurity can waylay the best of intentions. In Somalia, I felt as if I were on a moving train that I knew was going to crash, in spite of the project's quality organization and people.[65]

History

The strategic positioning of Somalia on the East coast of Africa is a critical point of importance when attempting to understand its turbulent history. Its geography is composed of Italy's former Trust Territory of Somalia and the former British Protectorate of Somaliland and its coastline extends over seventeen hundred miles.[66] Somalia's strategic geographic positioning drew interest from numerous European powers that began to establish a foothold for trade and influence in the region in the late 19th century. This struggle for power and influence continues today from within Somalia which affects global markets through modern piracy.

Somalia experienced a colonial period from 1891 to 1960 which divided the land into five parts which equally separated the people and their identities.[67] The early part of the twentieth century gave insight to the future of resistance from within when a rebellion led by Mohamed Abdullah challenged the British rule. The British bombed Abdullah's compound while rival Somali clans challenged his authority which led to his ultimate defeat.[68] His legend lives through the Somali People who consider him not only a hero, but a major figure of national identity. The concept of developing and maintaining national identity was especially difficult for the people of

---

[65] Ken Rutherford, *Humanitarianism Under Fire: The U.S. and UN Intervention in Somalia,* (Sterling, VA: Kumarian Press, 2008) 21.

[66] U.S. Department of State, "Background Note: Somalia," Bureau of African Affairs, http://www.state.gov/r/pa/ei/bgn/2863.htm#geo (accessed November 16, 2011).

[67] Robert F. Baumann, Lawrence A. Yates, and Versalle F. Washington. *My Clan Against the World: U.S. and Coalition Forces in Somalia 1992-1994* (Fort Leavenworth, KS: Combat Studies Institute Press, 2007), 11.

[68] U.S. Department of State, "Background Note: Somalia," Bureau of African Affairs, http://www.state.gov/r/pa/ei/bgn/2863.htm#geo (accessed November 16, 2011).

Somali at the conclusion of colonial rule. The Italian and British Colonial systems had left

Somalia divided with two distinct sets of laws, customs, economies, and languages.[69]

Somalia gained its independence from colonial rule and proceeded down the road of

unification on 1 July 1960.[70] It was at this point that the country adopted its first national

constitution in a countrywide referendum which set the foundation for a democratic state with a

parliamentary form of government based on European models.[71] A bloodless coup occurred on 21

October 1969, due to grievances toward government policy concerning the recognition of

borders. The change in national leadership resulted in the presidency of Maj. Gen. Mohamed Siad

Barre which effectively ended constitutional democracy in Somalia.[72] This point in Somalia's

history marks a distinct shift in internal and external interest bound by Cold War alliances.

President Barre shifted the internal political environment toward socialism and created a

Supreme Revolutionary Council (SRC).[73] The SRC streamlined governmental processes through

the advantage of unity and aligned itself ideologically and economically to the Soviet Union. This

obviously sparked the interest of the United States who in the midst of a cold war with the Soviet

Union would later be given an opportunity to create an alliance with Somalia. The SRC also

began to whittle away at the power of the clans who had traditionally handled necessities of

administration and governances.[74] The intent was to move Somalia from a decentralized nomadic

state to a modern state that could grow, compete, and prosper in the international arena. Somalia

harnessed the opportunity to benefit from Soviet friendship in the form of political alliance,

[69] Robert F. Baumann, Lawrence A. Yates, and Versalle F. Washington, *My Clan Against the World: U.S. and Coalition Forces in Somalia 1992-1994* (Fort Leavenworth, KS: Combat Studies Institute Press, 2007), 12.
[70] Ibid.
[71] U.S. Department of State, "Background Note: Somalia," Bureau of African Affairs, http://www.state.gov/r/pa/ei/bgn/2863.htm#geo (accessed November 16, 2011).
[72] Ibid.
[73] Robert F. Baumann, Lawrence A. Yates, and Versalle F. Washington, *My Clan Against the World: U.S. and Coalition Forces in Somalia 1992-1994* (Fort Leavenworth, KS: Combat Studies Institute Press, 2007), 13.
[74] Ibid.

military weaponry, and training. They would unfortunately find themselves in over their heads in the aftermath of the fall of the neighboring Ethiopian emperor.

As ambitions of the SRC on the international stage increased from 1970 on, tensions began to mount along the Somali-Ethiopian border.[75] Tensions increased in 1973 as the Mengistu Haile Mariam regime in Ethiopia assumed power. The new socialist aligned regime provided opportunity for the Soviet Union to increase its span of influence throughout the Horn of Africa. The Western Somali Liberation Front (WSLF) was soon created and began guerrilla operations in the previously disputed Ogaden region of Ethiopia.[76] The Ethiopian Emperor was overthrown in 1975 and Somalia invaded Ethiopia in 1977 in an attempt to regain the Ogaden region. After initial military success, Somalia failed to realize that the revolutionary Ethiopian Government had shifted its alliances from the West to the Soviet Union which coordinated Cuban troop support coupled with Soviet advisors.[77] This resulted in a shift of power and the ultimate defeat of Somalia in the region. Barre abruptly expelled all Soviet advisers in 1977 and abolished the alliance with the Soviet Union, but the damage was already done to Barre and his government.

After the Ogaden war, the United States capitalized on the opportunity to assist a country moving away from the USSR's sphere of influence and its socialist ideology in a search for a new partner and superpower alliance. During the Carter and Reagan administrations economic and military aid increased to over a hundred million dollars a year.[78] The aid continued until the collapse of the Barre regime by which time a surplus of military weaponry and training fell into

---

[75] U.S. Department of State, "Background Note: Somalia," Bureau of African Affairs, http://www.state.gov/r/pa/ei/bgn/2863.htm#geo (accessed November 16, 2011).
[76] Ibid.
[77] Ibid.
[78] Mohamed Sahnoun, *Somalia: The Missed Opportunities* (Washington D.C.: United States Institute of Peace Press, 1994), xiii.

the hands of the numerous warlords providing them the means to wage a brutal civil war.[79]

During the 1980s, Somalia became a key regional alley for the United States in its Cold War efforts. The United States increased its internal support while the Barre regime violently suppressed ethnic tensions and the development of opposition groups.[80] This led to internal turmoil for the government where conditions for civil war were ripe and the perception of the population as to who the U.S. government and U.S. military forces supported was clear.

Several separatist groups emerged beginning with the Somalia defeat in the Ogaden war. By 1979, a group of dissatisfied army officers created the Somali Salvation Democratic Front (SSDF). Another disparate group was formed in 1981 by the Isaaq clan due to increased angst with the Barre regime in the North. This group was labeled the Somali National Movement (SNM) whose stated goal was to overthrow the Barre regime.[81] As clans began to regain their sense of identity which was formally suppressed by the SRC, they also began to increase their influence and form formidable antigovernment movements. An additional group emerged in 1989 as the United Somali Congress (USC) which was an opposition group of Somalis from the Hawiye clan.[82] A military wing of the USC was formed in Ethiopia in late 1989 under the leadership of Mohamed Farah Aideed who was a former political prisoner imprisoned by Barre from 1969-75.[83] The USC built a coalition of alliances with other opposition groups and began to set the conditions for the destabilization of political and military power. President Barre's regime exacerbated the potential for destabilization by killing some 10,000 civilians and insurgents in the

---

[79] Robert F. Baumann, Lawrence A. Yates, and Versalle F. Washington, *My Clan Against the World: U.S. and Coalition Forces in Somalia 1992-1994* (Fort Leavenworth, KS: Combat Studies Institute Press, 2007), 5.

[80] U.S. Department of State, "Background Note: Somalia," Bureau of African Affairs, http://www.state.gov/r/pa/ei/bgn/2863.htm#geo (accessed November 16, 2011).

[81] Ibid.

[82] Ibid.

[83] Ibid.

city of Hargeisa in northwestern Somalia through airstrikes.[84] These attacks increased the instability in the country and helped set the conditions for civil war.

Another major contributor to the initiation of civil war was the economic crisis that developed due to numerous factors. One of these factors includes the mismanagement and looting of national funds by the Barre regime as the cost of combating numerous insurgent groups essentially bankrupted the country. The primary export of the country in the 1980s was cattle and livestock.[85] A major drought affected the production of their primary export and resulted in a seventy percent drop in output.[86] This potentially represented a missed opportunity by the United States in shaping their aid distribution as they essentially focused on rations and military aid to fight the insurgency rather than building economic capacity.

Barre's government began to lose control of the nation as insurgency movements spread throughout its borders. There were hundreds of thousands of refugees who fled to neighboring Ethiopia, Djibouti, and Kenya.[87] As the security situation began to further destabilize, the citizens of Somali returned to their respective clan militia which represented their true allegiance.[88] As the Barre government lost control of the country, external aid was reduced and effectively stopped from the United States as fears emerged concerning the use of any assistance. On the first week of December 1990, Barre declared a state of emergency as insurgent forces advanced toward Mogadishu.[89] In January 1991, Barre was driven out of power which resulted in the total collapse of the central government. In 1992, the United States and other nations launched Operation Restore Hope which was initiated to address the concern of extreme human suffering and reports

---

[84] U.S. Department of State, "Background Note: Somalia," Bureau of African Affairs, http://www.state.gov/r/pa/ei/bgn/2863.htm#geo (accessed November 16, 2011).
[85] Mohamed Sahnoun, *Somalia: The Missed Opportunities* (Washington DC: United States Institute of Peace Press, 1994), 15.
[86] Ibid.
[87] U.S. Department of State, "Background Note: Somalia," Bureau of African Affairs, http://www.state.gov/r/pa/ei/bgn/2863.htm#geo (accessed November 16, 2011).
[88] Ibid.
[89] Ibid.

29

of violations of human rights. A task force was created and was bolstered by additional international support from the United Nations Operation in Somalia (UNOSOM). The United States played a major role these operations and deployed over 10,000 troops.[90] On October 3-4, 1993, 18 U.S. servicemen were killed in an incident which prompted the removal of all U.S. forces in March of 1994.[91] Since then, U.S. involvement has been limited to temporary raids and drone strikes against Al Queda linked insurgent groups.

Critical Interest Related to U.S. National Interests

The historical background provides an initial perspective of the importance of Somalia to the United States and its strategic interests. Much like Liberia, there are geographic advantages to maintaining an influence in the region as well as international rights interests in the safety and wellbeing of its war ravaged population. In fact these two criteria alone are so similar that it is easy to see why so much time and money has been invested in both of these areas by the United States. These interests have increased today in the midst of a complex contemporary problem that includes piracy and the potential for international terrorist safe havens and training bases to exist in Somalia's ungoverned spaces.[92]

Somalia lies squarely on the coast of the Horn of Africa. American strategic interests in that area date back to the beginning of the Cold War. Somalia was swayed back and forth as an opportunist between the Soviet Union and the United States. As Liberia served as a base station for positional navigation across the vast Atlantic Ocean as well as a relay for communications

---

[90] Robert F. Baumann, Lawrence A. Yates, and Versalle F. Washington, *My Clan Against the World: U.S. and Coalition Forces in Somalia 1992-1994* (Fort Leavenworth, KS: Combat Studies Institute Press, 2007), 5.

[91] U.S. Department of State, "Background Note: Somalia," Bureau of African Affairs, http://www.state.gov/r/pa/ei/bgn/2863.htm#geo (accessed November 16, 2011).

[92] Kenneth J. Menkhaus, "State Fragility as a Wicked Problem," *Prism* 1, no. 2 (2009): 85-100.

across Africa, Somalia served as a listening post on the opposite end of the continent.[93] As the

United States lost regional influence of the area due to persistent armed conflict since 1988, the

area gave way to contemporary threats of piracy and terrorist basing.[94]

The loss of influence began to erode after the oppressive Barre regime was challenged by

armed opposition. This led to the increase of extreme human suffering in the form of war and

famine. The United States decided to intervene along with the United Nations in what became the

UNOSOM mission. This is an interesting shift in interests from the Cold War era of bolstering

the government of Somalia's ability to defend itself through massive amounts of military aid and

training to one of halting the violence that was enabled by those previous efforts.[95] "The United

States gave Barre $100 million per year in development and direct military aid. This aid

continued until the Barre government's collapse and was supplemented with aid from Saudi

Arabia, China, South Africa, and other nations. All of this military aid would find its way into the

hands of various warlords, providing them with the means for waging their civil war."[96] This

paradoxical dilemma would later manifest itself into additional future problems for the United

States and the world in the form of piracy.

Contemporary interests in Somalia are similar to the past in terms of geography and the

protection of human rights; however, new problems emerged in the form of terrorism and piracy.

"Hence, piracy is usually presented as a symptom of "state collapse" and a breeding ground for

global jihad, while its moral economy is disqualified and the reconfiguration of a transnational

---

[93] Richard Stewart, *The United States Army in Somalia, 1992-1994* (Washington, D.C.: U.S. Army Center of Military History, 2003), 3.

[94] Kenneth J. Menkhaus, "State Fragility as a Wicked Problem," *Prism* 1, no. 2 (2009): 28.

[95] Robert F. Baumann, Lawrence A. Yates, and Versalle F. Washington. *My Clan Against the World: U.S. and Coalition Forces in Somalia 1992-1994* (Fort Leavenworth, KS: Combat Studies Institute Press, 2007), 15.

[96] Ibid.

Somali economy simply ignored."[97] This illustrates that the current state of affairs in Somalia is due in part to the lack of a legitimate economic system in the country. U.S. strategic interests have evolved since the cold war and have transitioned from ambitions of regional control through the use of economic and military aid to the relief of suffering through the distribution of humanitarian relief. Unfortunately, this indirect approach has not lead to a viable solution to the issue of instability and human suffering.

Economic Inquiries

The first question remains, "Who leads or influences economic change in the conflict, and are those efforts aligned with U.S. national interest? "The primary export of the Somalia economy throughout the 1980s was cattle.[98] This continues to be the major contributor to their legitimate economy along with telecommunications.[99] The cattle market was decimated throughout the 1980s and 1990s due to war, drought, and disease. Over seventy percent of the market was lost during the tumultuous ending of the Barre regime.[100] This contributed to increased conditions of unrest which eventually cascaded into civil war. The Barre regime began to drain the nation's economic resources by funding a counterinsurgency while ignoring the development and sustainment of their core economic export. The local economy was further injured through government corruption and the hording of power and resources by those in control of the government. This led to the intervention of United States and its efforts to address the massive amounts of human suffering through UNOSOM.

---

[97] Roland Marchal, "Somali-piracy Local Contexts International Obsession," *Humanity Journal* 2, no. 1(February 2011), http://www.humanityjournal.org/humanity-volume-2-issue-1/somali-piracy-local-contexts-international-obsession (accessed November 16, 2011).

[98] Mohamed Sahnoun, *Somalia: The Missed Opportunities* (Washington D.C.: United States Institute of Peace Press, 1994), 15.

[99] Central Intelligence World Factbook, "Somalia," Factbook, https://www.cia.gov/library /publications /the-world-factbook/ (accessed December 3, 2011).

[100] Mohamed Sahnoun, *Somalia: The Missed Opportunities* (Washington D.C.: United States Institute of Peace Press, 1994), 15.

"Crisis of vast proportions and we're paying the price for past neglect."[101] This describes the conditions just before and during the U.S. intervention. Their effort to set the conditions to provide humanitarian aid and distribution ended a bloody exchange of violence between warlords and U.S. military personnel. Unfortunately, the efforts of UNOSOM were focused on distribution of aid rather than security and the stability of the environment. While there were numerous international aid organizations attempting to help and improve the overall conditions, their efforts were governed by the instability and lack of security. These agencies' effect on the local economy was severely limited and complicated by the decentralized manner by which they applied their efforts and resources. The uncontrollable violence led to the withdrawal of all U.S. forces and left the country to its own demise.

In Somalia the second question of how economic advisors were integrated into stability operations and what was their degree of influence was difficult to answer. Conditions in this country suffered from a long history of instability. Integration of advisors proved more than difficult due to the instability and lack of security. While the United States attempted to inject stability to the growing humanitarian crisis with military forces, the limited *understanding of the environment* and local *perception* prevented successful integration of advisors. As U.S. forces were mobilized to intervene and skip straight to the task to provide humanitarian relief, Kenneth R. Rutherford, in reflection, asks the question "Why did President George H. W. Bush send more than 30,000 troops in late 1992 to Somalia when there was neither security nor international norms at stake?"[102] The lack of security in this case may have led to a *perception* by the local

---

[101] Mohamed Sahnoun, *Somalia: The Missed Opportunities* (Washington D.C.: United States Institute of Peace Press, 1994), 28.

[102] Ken Rutherford, *Humanitarianism Under Fire: The U.S. and UN Intervention in Somalia* (Sterling, VA: Kumarian Press, 2008), xv.

Somalis that the military was not there to help when needed. They were essentially too late which in turn helped feed the escalating cycle of violence.

The inevitable demise of the Somali government as perceived by the U.S. government took an interesting path that deviated from expectations. The famous metaphor coined by economist Adam Smith of "the invisible hand" took effect after the extraction of external military forces. After 1993, there is evidence of free market initiatives that harnessed individual ambition which ultimately benefited the tribal assemblies. The increase in foreign investment in telecommunications is a good example of a free market at work to improve itself. The CIA estimated the gross domestic product (GDP) at $3.3 billion in 1994 which grew over time to an estimated $4.1 billion in 2001.[103] By 2009, the GDP had grown to $5.7 billion which includes private sector investment.[104] This increase is due in part to the elimination of the Barre regime that formerly controlled all services and the industrial sector. The fall of the central government appeared to actually help the local economy in the long run; however, a new threat emerged due to a lack of effective governance that provided opportunity for illegal activities such as piracy.

The final question is "What are the unintended consequences (second and third order effects) of military led economic development?" Current scholars postulate that "a case can be made that attempts to revive a central state structure have actually exacerbated armed conflicts. State-building and peace-building are, in this view, two separate and in some respects mutually antagonistic enterprises. This is because the revival of a state structure is viewed in Somali corners as a zero sum game."[105] This view highlights the requirement for not only a clear political objective but most importantly from a military perspective, a clear end state. The use of the same uniformed military forces that were used to facilitate training and arms distribution during the

---

[103] Central Intelligence World Factbook, "Somalia," Factbook, https://www.cia.gov/library /publications /the-world-factbook/ (accessed December 3, 2011).
[104] Ibid.
[105] Kenneth J. Menkhaus, "State Fragility as a Wicked Problem," *Prism* 1, no. 2 (2009): 18.

Cold War and Barre regime struggled to provide security and enable humanitarian distribution. This was clearly complicated by the *perception* of external support to the address what the local powerbrokers and warlords believed was an internal problem. The fragility of this *perception* was highlighted in 1992 when additional United Nations troop support authorization were increased from 500 troops to over 3,000 troops without the consultation of Somali leaders, community elders, or the neighboring countries.[106] An additional incident occurred when a Russian military transport plane flying under the markings and contract of the United Nations flew a supply of aid and weapons to interim president Ali Mahdi.[107] This infuriated arch-rival Aideed and succeeded in planting doubt in the minds of the locals in terms of the agenda carried by the outside world.

A perfect storm of violence emerged when the height of U.S. forces were employed in 1993 to help relieve humanitarian suffering. Distrust from tribal leaders and warlords whose influence spilled over adjacent borders emerged to spite the efforts of organized humanitarian relief operations. This distrust manifested itself into extreme violence which led to U.S. policy change that led to a new policy and strategic approach. After the deaths of 18 Army Rangers in Mogadishu, the United States completely withdrew its humanitarian efforts and engaged in a strategy of disengagement and self-fulfillment.[108]

---

[106] Mohamed Sahnoun, *Somalia: The Missed Opportunities* (Washington D.C.: United States Institute of Peace Press, 1994), 38.

[107] Ibid.

[108] Paolo Tripodi, *The Colonial Legacy in Somalia: Rome and Mogadishu: from Colonial Administration to Operation Restore Hope* (Basingstoke: Macmillan, 1999), 212.

Conclusion

There are two clear trends that emerge from the examination of the case studies in Liberia and Somalia. These trends provide insight to the viability of the U.S. Military's conduct of Expeditionary Economics. The first is the neglect or inability to fully *understand the operational environment.* This is a clear trend that manifests itself in after action reports from not only the lessons of Liberia and Somalia, but many other conflicts where U.S. forces have conducted operations. The second is more evasive and relates to the *perception* of the local population. This specifically refers to the historical interaction of U.S. military forces with a local population who experienced periods of relative stability followed by great hardships and war.

The ability to understand the operational environment is critical in any military operation. The additional weight of spearheading expeditionary economic efforts placed squarely on the shoulders of the U.S. military limits the ability of that organization to experience decisive efforts. Discussions must address concerns of which type of economic strategy is best for the given environment. This discussion could teeter from a Keynesian approach that supports government intervention as necessary to ensure the overall health of the economy to a Friedman strategy where the local leadership advocates for free markets and rejects the use of fiscal policy as a healthy government action. While there are currently no references to any type of economic strategy in current U.S. military doctrine, the *Stability Operations Manual (FM 3-07)* discusses the requirement to provide security and enable essential needs and services.

Fledgling economies in war torn regions such as Liberia and Somalia are difficult to understand without first taking the time to address basic needs of the local population such as security. While this may appear to be obvious, Kennith J. Menkhaus adds an additional twist to understanding the local environment from both the general population and the key leaders whom military forces would interact with to apply expeditionary economics. He suggests that "State fragility may be seen by key local leaders as an acceptable or even optimal solution, not a problem to be solved."[109] If this is indeed the goal of local leadership in places such as Liberia and Somalia, then perhaps the assumptions made by U.S. military and political leaders are invalid and the problem needs to be reframed and addressed appropriately.

While local powerbrokers may welcome instability, U.S. national policy efforts attempt to reconcile the problem with a disproportional application of diplomatic, information, military, and economic initiatives. This was the case in Somalia in the early 1990s where the United States attempted to provide humanitarian relief to the war torn region, but only succeeded in intensifying the violence. This is a clear example of limited understanding of the operational environment by the United States Government. Ariel I. Ahram addresses an additional point of friction in the environment where he finds that "literature on new wars suggests that state complicity in the perpetuation of war in pursuit of parochial economic interests is not rare."[110] The same local leadership that military forces are engaged with to cooperate economic initiatives could in fact be part of the hidden problem in the environment.

This hidden problem perpetuated itself in Liberia through two periods of civil war. The market economy was focused on one or two primary commodities which complicated the promise of economic expansion through expeditionary means. The two commodities were iron ore and rubber whose industries were heavily subsidized by United States public and private initiatives. A continuation of War in that region actually benefited local powerbrokers at the expense of thousands of innocent civilians by allowing them to focus their control of the limited market. Part of the U.S. government involvement prior to the civil wars in Liberia included large amounts of foreign military assistance which contained large quantities of military weapons sales. These

---

[109] Kenneth J. Menkhaus, "State Fragility as a Wicked Problem," *Prism* 1, no. 2 (2009): 89.
[110] Ariel I. Ahram, *Proxy Warriors: The Rise and Fall of State-Sponsored Militias* (Stanford, CA: Stanford Security Studies, 2011), 15.

weapons sales coupled with overt military training helped create a *perception* of U.S. military involvement and their motives in the region.

The *perception* of U.S. military forces operating within the boundaries of a sovereign state is the second derivative of the case study analysis. Walter McDougal discusses U.S. policy as interventionism where the United States is a force for bettering the world as a crusader state with the mission to bring democracy, freedom, and human rights to less fortunate nations.[111] This is based on the historical evolution of U.S. foreign policy and is not easily masked by the deployment of military forces to a nation in turmoil. One of the most problematic barriers to overcome is the *perceived* intent of U.S. military forces. Their history in Liberia included arming and training legitimate government forces who subsequently defected and some of whom led coups against the government which resulted in mass human suffering.

Military sales programs and training programs have second and third order affects that could support or enable government overthrows and secular violence such as those cases in Liberia and Somalia. These military led actions develop a perception of directly or indirectly supporting civil wars. Current U.S. military efforts may fall victim to a localized *perception* that may precede any individual or formation of troops on the ground. While the U.S. government has diplomatic, information, military, and economic tools to choose from to address a problem, the military is perhaps the most inappropriate tool to address economic development in areas where their intent is shaped by a preexisting perception.

Inaccurate and limited *understandings of the local operational environment* coupled with local *perceptions* anchored by history are realities faced by expeditionary military forces. The risks that emerge to the mission are further compounded by increasing the role of military forces to include expeditionary economics. The complexities of local economies lead soldier statesmen

---

[111] Walter McDougall, *Promised Land, Crusader State: the American Encounter with the World Since 1776* (Boston: Houghton Mifflin, 1998).

38

down a dangerous path that may take a sharp departure from their core competencies. Huntington describes these important competencies as complex skills needed to manage violence.[112] There is a clear need to create or bolster economic initiatives in war torn regions in order to help stabilize a region; however, the tools used by the U.S. government must be sorely scrutinized. The U.S. military would benefit greatly from the council of a trained economic advisor embedded at the ground level. This advisor could help leaders *understand the environment* and develop a well nested plan that compliments U.S. national policy that remains within the realm of their professional means.

---

[112] Huntington, *The Soldier and the State*, 12.

Appendix

Economic Definitions

There are numerous economic managerial methods; however, common language provides a foundation for which to discuss application of the best approach. The following is a list of terms and concepts that are common to such discussions:

Command Process: The use of central planning and the directives of government authorities to answer the question of what, how, and for whom.

Economic decisions for the firm: What goods and services should be produced? – the product decision. How should these goods and services be produced? – the hiring, staffing, and capital-budgeting decision. For whom should these goods and services be produced?

Economics: The study of how choices are made under conditions of scarcity. The basic economic problem that can be defined as: "What goods and services should be produced?" "For whom should these goods and services be produced?"

Microeconomics: The study of individual consumers and producers in specific markets. This includes supply and demand in individual markets, the pricing of specific outputs and inputs, production and cost structures for individual goods and services, and the distribution of income and output in the population.

Macroeconomics: The study of the aggregate economy. This includes analysis of the gross domestic product, unemployment, inflation, fiscal and monetary policy, and the trade and financial relationships among nations.

Economics of a business: The key factors that affect the ability of a firm to earn an acceptable rate of return on its owners' investment. The most important of these factors are competition, technology, and customers.

40

Managerial economics: The use of economic analysis to make business decisions involving the best use of a firm's scarce resources.

Market process: The use of supply, demand, and material incentives to answer the question of what, how, and for whom.

Opportunity Cost: The amount or subjective value forgone in choosing one activity over the next best alternative. This cost must be considered whenever decisions are made under conditions of scarcity.

Resources: Also referred to as factors of production or inputs, economic analysis usually includes four basic types: land, labor, capital, and entrepreneurship.

Scarcity: A condition that exists when resources are limited relative to the demand of their use. In the market process, the extent of this condition is reflected in the price of resources or the goods and services they produce.

Traditional process: The use of customs and traditions to answer the questions of what, how, and for whom.

Liberia's Civil War Facts

- Liberia is staggering under an external debt of $3.7 billion, a per capita GDP that is estimated to have declined 90 per cent from U.S.$1,269 in 1980 to $163 in 2005, and an unemployment rate of over 80 per cent.

- There are no functioning public utilities, and the vast majority of Liberians have no access to electricity, water and basic sanitation facilities, or health care. Almost all medical services are provided by international non-governmental organizations and UN agencies.

- Roads and bridges, which are needed to open up markets, increase employment, sustain humanitarian access to rural areas and expand the overall protection environment, are in dire need of repairs. While UNMIL engineers and members of the UN country team have undertaken rehabilitation work on important road networks to facilitate the return of internally displaced persons and refugees, much more remains to be done.

- The education system is dilapidated, with a dearth of qualified teachers and available resources to rehabilitate school buildings.

- Liberia has no effectively functioning judicial system; outside of the capital, Monrovia, most courts have been destroyed and trial-by-ordeal is not unheard of. The culture of impunity that has developed in the absence of justice must be replaced by respect for human rights and the rule of law.

- During the civil war the country's human resources suffered from a 'brain drain' and crisis-related deaths. Vital socio-economic infrastructure was swept away as bad governance, embezzlement, smuggling out of natural resources and economic mismanagement took their toll.

- At the end of civil war, there were 314,000 registered internally displaced persons (IDPs) in the country and 340,000 refugees registered with UNHCR in neighbouring countries. While the UN-backed return process for IDPs came to an end in April 2006 and the majority of the refugees have returned to the country, the job of resettlement continues as returnees struggle to rebuild their lives and communities.

Acronyms

AAB – Advise and Assist Brigade

AC – Active Component

ACS – Advanced Civil Schooling

ARFORGEN – Army Force Generation Model

ASI – Army Skill Identifier

BCT – Brigade Combat Team

BDE – Brigade

BOG – Boots on the Ground

CA – Civil Affairs

CARD – Center for Agriculture and Rural Development

CCC – Captains Career Course

CCJO – Capstone Concept for Joint Operations

CCP – Contingency Command Post

CGSC – Command and General Staff College

CERP – Commander's Emergency Relief Program

DoD – Department of Defense

ePRT – Embedded Provincial Reconstruction Teams

FM – Field Manual

GCC – Global Combatant Command

HBCT – Heavy Brigade Combat Teams

ILE – Intermediate Level Training

JOE – Joint Operating Environment

NDS – National Defense Strategy

NGO – Non-Government Organization

NSS – National Security Strategy

OBC – Officer Basic Course

OEF – Operation Enduring Freedom

OIF – Operation Iraqi Freedom

PRT – Provincial Reconstruction Teams

QDR – Quadrennial Defense Review

RC – Reserve Component

S/CRS – Department of State Office of the Coordinator for Reconstruction and

Stabilization

ULO – Unified Land Operations

U.S.AID – U.S. Agency for International Development

U.S.AFRICOM – U.S. Africa Command

U.S.AR – U.S. Army Reserve

U.S.CENTCOM – U.S. Central Command

U.S.EUCOM – U.S. European Command

U.S.PACOM – U.S. Pacific Command

U.S.SOUTHCOM – U.S. Southern Command

Bibliography

Ahram, Ariel I. *Proxy Warriors: The Rise and Fall of State-Sponsored Militias*. Stanford, CA: Stanford Security Studies, 2011.

Baumann, Robert F., Lawrence A. Yates, and Versalle F. Washington. *My Clan Against the World: U.S. and Coalition Forces in Somalia 1992-1994*. Fort Leavenworth, KS: Combat Studies Institute Press, 2007.

Blinder, Alan S. "Keynsian Economics: The Concise Encyclopedia of Economics," *The Library of Economics and Liberty*. http://www.econlib.org/library/Enc/KeynesianEconomics.html (accessed November 16, 2011).

Bruton, Bronwyn E. "Somalia A New Approach." *Council on Foreign Relations*, no. 52 (March 2010): 1-45.

Butler, E. *Milton Friedman: A Guide To His Economic Thought*. New York: Universe, 1985.

Cobban, A. *The Nation State and National Self- Determination*. New York: Stephen Y. Cromwell, 1970.

Dobbins, James. *America's Role in Nation-Building from Germany to Iraq*. Santa Monica, CA: Rand, 2003.

Dolman, Everett C. *Pure Strategy: Power and Principle in the Space and Information Age*. New York: Frank Cass, 2005.

Dunn, Elwood D., Svend E. Holsoe. *Historical Dictionary of Liberia*. London: The Scarecrow Press, 1985.

Ellis, Stephen. *The Mask of Anarchy: The Destruction of Liberia and the Religious Dimension of an African Civil War*. New York: New York University Press, 1999.

Ewing Marion Kauffman Foundation. "Expeditionary Economics: Economic Growth, Security, and Stability in Conflict and Disaster Areas." The Kauffman Foundation. http://kauffman.org/researchandpolicy/expeditionary-economics.aspx (accessed August 3, 2011)

Fisher, I. *Elementary Principles of Economics*. General Books LLC, 2010.

Friedman, M. *Essays in Positive Economics*. Chicago: The University of Chicago Press, 1953.

Friedman, Milton & Rose. *Two Lucky People: Memoirs*, Chicago: The University of Chicago Press, 1998.

George, Alexander L., Andrew Bennett. *Case Studies and Theory Development in the Social Sciences*. Cambridge: MIT Press, 2005.

Hayek, F. *The Road to Serfdom*. Chicago: The University of Chicago Press, 2007.

Heads of State and Government of the Member States of the Economic Community of West African States (ECOWAS). "ECOWAS Treaty," http://www.worldtradelaw.net/fta/agreements/ecowasfta.pdf (accessed November 16,2011).

Howard, Michael, Peter Paret. *Carl Von Clausewitz: On War*. New Jersey: Princeton University Press, 1976.

Huband, Mark. *The Liberian Civil War*. London: Frank Cass Publishers, 1998.

Huntington, Samuel P. *The Soldier and the State*. New York, N.Y.: Vintage Books, 1957.

Kaplan, Robert D. "The Coming Anarchy," *The Atlantic Monthly*, February 1994: 44-68.

Keynes, J. *The Economic Consequences of Peace*. Toronto: University of Toronto Libraries, 2011.

Keynes, J.M. The General Theory of Emplyment, Interst, and Money. New York: Harcourt, Brace, & World, Inc., 1935.

Kotter, John P. Power and Influence. New York: Free Press, 1985.

Marchal, Roland. "Somali-piracy Local Contexts International Obsession." *Humanity Journal* 2, no. 1(February 2011). http://www.humanityjournal.org/humanity-volume-2-issue-1/somali-piracy-local-contexts-international-obsession (accessed November 16, 2011).

McConnell, Campbell R. and Stanley L. Brue, *Economics: Principles, Problems, and Policies*. New York: McGraw-Hill, 2004.

McDonald, P. *The Invisible Hand of Peace: Capitalism, The War Machine, and International Relations Theory*. New York: Cambridge, 2009.

McDougall, Walter. *Promised Land, Crusader State: the American Encounter with the World Since 1776*. Boston: Houghton Mifflin, 1998.

Menkhaus, Kenneth J. "State Fragility as a Wicked Problem." *Prism*1, no. 2 (2009): 85-100.

Modigliani, F. *The Debate Over Stabilization Policy (Raffaele Matticli Lectures)*. Cambridge: Cambridge University Press, 1986.

Molavi, A. "The New Silk Road" The Washington Post (April 9, 2007). http://www. washingtonpost.com/wp-dyn/content/article/2007/04/08/AR2007040800923. html (accessed August 3, 2011).

Muller, Jerry Z. *Adam Smith in his Time and Ours*, New York: Free Press, 1993.

Murray, Williamson, and Major General Robert H. Scales. *The Iraq War*. Cambridge: Belknap Press, 2003.

Nelson, Harold D. *Liberia: A Country Study*, Washington, DC: Foreign Area Studies The American University, 1984.

Noland, Marcus and Howard Pack. *The Arab Economies in a Changing World*. Washington: Peter G. Peterson Institute for International Economics, 2007.

Nmoma, V. "Power and Force: Libya's Relations with the United States." *Journal of Third World Studies* 26, no. 2 (October 1, 2009): 137-159. http://www.proquest.com (accessed October 6, 2011)

Paris, Roland. *At War's End: Building Peace After Civil Conflict*. New York: Cambridge University Press, 2004.

PBS. "Liberia's Uneasy Peace." Economic Community of West African States. http://www.pbs.org/newshour/bb/africa/liberia/ecowas-background.html (accessed November 16, 2011).

Peters, G. *Seeds of Terror: How Heroin is Bankrolling the Taliban and al Qaeda*. New York: Thomas Dunne Books, 2009.

Pham, John-Peter. *Liberia: Portrait of a Failed State*. New York: Reed Press, 2004.

Rutherford, Ken. *Humanitarianism Under Fire: the U.S. and UN Intervention in Somalia*. Sterling, VA: Kumarian Press, 2008.

Sahnoun, Mohamed. *Somalia: The Missed Opportunities*. Washington DC: United States Institute of Peace Press, 1994.

Salman, G. *Poppy: Life, Death and Addiction Inside Afghanistans Opium Trade*. New York: Random House, 2009.

Sawyer, Amos. *The Emergency of Autocracy in Liberia: Tragedy and Challenge*. San Francisco, CA: Institute for Contemporary Studies, 1992.

Schramm, C. J. "Expeditionary Economics." *Foreign Affairs* (2010, May/June): 89-99.

Shultz, Tammy S. Preparing for an Era of Persistent Conflict. Quantica, VA: Marine Corps University, 2011.

Sorley, Lewis. *A Better War: The Unexamined Victories and Final Tragedy of America's Last Years in Vietnam*. Orlando, FL: Harvest Book Hartcourt, Inc., 2008.

Spiegel, Henry William. *The Growth of Economic Thought*, Washington DC: Library of Congress, 1991.

Stevenson, Johnathan. *Losing Mogadishu: Testing U.S. Policy in Somalia*. Annapolis, MD: Naval Institute Press, 1995.

Stewart, Richard. *The United States Army in Somalia, 1992-1994*. Washington, DC: U.S. Army Center of Military History, 2003.

Tripodi, Paolo. *The Colonial Legacy in Somalia: Rome and Mogadishu: from Colonial Administration to Operation Restore Hope*. Basingstoke: Macmillan, 1999.

The Economist. "War and Peace in Monrovia." The Economist Library, http://www.economist. com/blogs/prospero/2012/02/war-and-peace-monrovia?fsrc=gn_ep (accessed November 16, 2011).

U.S. Army, *Army Doctrinal Publication 3-0, Unified Land Operations.* Washington, DC: Headquarters, Department of the Army, 2011.

———— *Field Manual (FM) 3-07, Stability Operations.* Washington, DC: Headquarters, Department of the Army, 2009.

———— *Field Manual (FM) 5-19, Composite Risk Management.* Washington, DC: Headquarters, Department of the Army, 2006.

U.S. Department of State. "Background Note: Liberia." Bureau of African Affairs. http://www.state.gov/r/pa/ei/bgn/6618.htm (accessed November 16, 2011).

————"Background Note: Somalia." Bureau of African Affairs, http://www.state.gov/r/pa/ei/bgn/2863.htm#geo (accessed November 16, 2011).

U.S. General Accounting Office. *Peace Operations: Cost of DOD Operations in Somalia. Washington DC:* Government Printing Office, 1994.

United Nations Mission in Liberia. "Liberia: Development Challenges to Agenda as the Nation Recovers from Years of Civil Strife." United Nations. http://www.un.org/events/tenstories/06/story.asp? storyID=2100 (accessed November 16, 2011).

Watson, B. C. "Reshaping the Expeditionary Army To Win Decisively: The Case For Greater Stabilization Capacity in the Modular Force." Strategic Studies Institute, 2005.

Wilson, Charles Morrow. *Liberia: Black Africa in Microcosm.* New York: Harper and Row Publishers, 1971.

Wright, David McCord. *The Keynesian System.* New York: Fordham University Press, 1961.

Yergin, Daniel, Joseph Stanislaw. *The Commanding Heights: The Battle for the World Economy.* New York: Free Press, 1998.

www.ingramcontent.com/pod-product-compliance
Lightning Source LLC
Chambersburg PA
CBHW080614290526

45790CB00007B/2777